D0513836

Harry Ramsden's
A TASTE OF TRADITION

Harry Ramsden's
A TASTE OF TRADITION

Tessa Bramley

HarperCollins*Publishers*

First published in 1997 by
HarperCollins*Publishers*
77-85 Fulham Palace Road, London W6 8JB

Recipe text © Tessa Bramley 1997

1 3 5 7 9 8 6 4 2

A CIP catalogue record for this book
is available from the British Library.

ISBN 0 00 414014 1

Commissioning Editor: Barbara Dixon
Editor: Becky Humphreys
Designer: Rachel Smyth
Illustrator: Neil Bulpitt

Front photograph: Fritz von der Schulenburg/
The Interior Archive

Printed and bound by Bath Press, Bath, UK

About the author

Tessa Bramley is chef and patron of the highly acclaimed Old Vicarage restaurant at the village of Ridgeway in Derbyshire, which she runs with the help of her son. She was awarded two stars by the *Egon Ronay 1996 Guide* – one of only six restaurants to achieve this status outside London. Tessa is a self-taught chef, whose food is bursting with flavour. It is real country cooking, made with the freshest of ingredients, many of the vegetables, herbs and fruits coming from her own kitchen garden.

Kit Chapman devoted a chapter to Tessa, her life and her cooking, in his book *Great British Chefs 2*. Tessa was a regular presenter on Here's One I Made Earlier, and has appeared on This Morning with Robert Carrier. Her first book, *The Instinctive Cook*, was published in Autumn 1994.

Notes on the recipes

All recipes serve 4 people unless otherwise stated.

When making any of the recipes in this book,
follow only one set of measures as they are not interchangeable.

All eggs are size 2 unless otherwise stated.

Always chop fresh herbs just before required,
to ensure maximum flavour.

Use unwaxed fruits whenever possible; if the fruits are waxed,
wash and scrub them well and dry before use.

CONTENTS

THE STORY OF

Harry Ramsden's

*I*t was on 20th December 1928, with only £150, that Harry Ramsden founded what was to become the world's most famous fish and chip restaurant in Guiseley, near Leeds. It was a modest beginning in a small, green and white painted wooden hut, which you can still see on the site to this day.

The first customers were probably ramblers, cyclists and passengers from the Leeds and Bradford tram terminus. The word soon spread regarding Harry's delicious fish and chips and business quickly flourished. Inspired by this success, Harry embarked on an ambitious plan to build the biggest and best fish and chip restaurant in the country. He borrowed £2,000 each from his potato dealer, fish supplier and fat supplier and in 1931 Harry Ramsden's as we know it today was built.

With chandeliers, linen table cloths and silver vases, Harry Ramsden's is no ordinary fish and chip shop. The million customers that flock to Harry Ramsden's each year love the unique atmosphere of the restaurant, but the main reason for Harry Ramsden's success is they always serve the tastiest fish and chips.

Harry Ramsden's have taken the principles of their founder and have opened restaurants throughout the world. All the restaurants have been modelled on the original Guiseley restaurant, and serve the same, traditional favourites.

Harry Ramsden's A Taste of Tradition is a nostalgic look at British food, customs and traditions as Harry would have known them. It includes recipes for fish dishes (of course!), but also includes other favourites from the time, many of which you will recognise, while others will be less familiar.

STARTERS

Leek and Mushroom Soup with Croutons

Pumpkin, Honey and Ginger Soup

Fillet of Halibut with Rhubarb Butter Sauce

Roast Salmon Fillet with Sorrel Sauce

Potted Morecambe Bay Shrimps

Steamed Mussels and Scallions in a Cream and Rosemary Sauce

Pickled Squab Pigeon with Walnut Oil

Salad of Chicken Livers with Beetroot Dressing

Devilled Kidneys on Parsnip Purée

Leek and Mushroom Soup with Croutons

55g/2oz unsalted butter

450g/1lb leeks, trimmed and sliced

175g/6oz button mushrooms, sliced

1 stick celery, chopped

1 onion, chopped

1.2 litres/2 pints water

salt and freshly ground black pepper

3 or 4 sprigs fresh thyme

300ml/½ pint double cream

1 fat garlic clove

4 thick slices of white bread, crusts removed

4 or 5 tablespoons olive oil

1 Melt the butter in a large, heavy pan and sweat the vegetables for 2-3 minutes. They should soften without colouring.

2 Add the water, seasoning and thyme. Bring to the boil. Reduce the heat and simmer for about 20 minutes until the vegetables are tender.

3 Remove the thyme and discard. Liquidise the soup and pass through a coarse sieve to remove any unwanted stringy bits.

4 Rinse out the pan and return the soup to it. Stir in the cream and reheat gently. Check the seasoning and adjust if necessary.

5 Cut the garlic clove in half and rub over the surface of the bread slices. Cut the bread into small cubes.

6 Preheat a heavy based frying pan and heat the oil until hot and hazy. Fry the bread cubes, turning them frequently until golden and crisp. Remove with a slotted spoon and drain on kitchen paper. Serve the soup, piping hot, with a generous sprinkling of croutons.

Pumpkin, Honey and Ginger Soup

Children love the atmosphere of Hallowe'en and what could be nicer to warm them up after an evening trick-and-treating than this delicious pumpkin soup? You could round off the meal with apple bobbing!

55g/2oz unsalted butter
450g/1lb pumpkin flesh, chopped
1 small onion, chopped
1 stick celery, chopped
2 large nodules of fresh ginger, chopped
1 fat garlic clove, chopped
900ml/1½ pints water
2 teaspoons wild flower honey
salt and freshly ground black pepper
150ml/5fl oz double cream
1 tablespoon chopped fresh chives to garnish

1 Melt the butter in a large pan, and fry the vegetables and ginger, gently, until soft but not coloured.

2 Add the garlic, water, honey and seasoning and bring to the boil. Simmer gently until the vegetables are tender.

3 Reserve 1 tablespoon of cream and add the rest to the soup and reheat gently. Check the seasoning and adjust if necessary.

4 Serve in soup bowls, swirling in the reserved cream with the tip of a knife. Garnish with the chopped chives.

A very large shopping list

Most of the menu served in Harry Ramsden's today is the same as when Harry Ramsden's first opened. The annual shopping list for Guiseley includes: 264,000lbs of haddock; 660,000lbs of potatoes; 6,500 bottles of vinegar; 20,000 bottles of sauce and 360,000 tea bags.

Fillet of Halibut with Rhubarb Butter Sauce

450g/1lb young forced rhubarb, sliced

1 teaspoon caster sugar

1 tablespoon water

150ml/5fl oz fish stock

3 pieces star anise

salt and freshly ground black pepper

25g/1oz unsalted butter, chilled

450g/1lb halibut, filleted

150ml/5fl oz white wine and water mixed (about half and half)

1 First make the sauce. Cook the rhubarb in a pan with the sugar and water, until puréed.

2 Bring the fish stock to the boil in another pan and reduce by half. Add the puréed rhubarb, 2 pieces of star anise and season. Simmer for 2-3 minutes then pass through a sieve into a clean pan.

3 Over a gentle heat, whisk in the chilled butter to give a good gloss. Check the seasoning and add a little extra sugar if necessary. Be careful to keep the sauce warm, not hot, as overheating will spoil its colour.

4 Skin the halibut and cut into four pieces. Season, and lay each piece on a sheet of foil 2½ times its size. Fold the foil over the fish to make a parcel and seal two short sides, leaving a small gap.

5 Crush the remaining piece of star anise into the wine and water mixture and pour into the parcels. Seal the parcels firmly.

6 Place the foil parcels on a baking sheet and cook in preheated oven at 220°C/425°F/Gas 7 for 4-6 minutes, depending on the thickness of the fish. When cooked, the fish will feel firm to the touch and will have a pearly, opaque look.

7 Pour the juices from the parcels into the rhubarb sauce. Taste and adjust the seasoning and whisk in a little more butter if necessary. Pour the sauce around the halibut to serve.

Roast Salmon Fillet with Sorrel Sauce

At its best in Spring, rod-caught wild salmon with sorrel sauce is a timeless classic. Cooked like this, the salmon is crisp outside, meltingly tender and moist inside, and contrasts beautifully with the fresh flavour of the sorrel. Sorrel is easy to grow yourself, but nowadays can be found in most good supermarkets.

450g/1lb salmon fillet, skinned and boned

salt and freshly ground black pepper

2 tablespoons extra virgin olive oil

300ml/10fl oz fish stock

squeeze of fresh lemon juice

1 piece star anise

75g/3oz unsalted butter, chilled

large handful of fresh sorrel leaves

sugar to taste

1 Cut the salmon fillet into 4 pieces. Season and rub the top side of the salmon with olive oil.

2 Heat a cast iron pan or a griddle until evenly hot and sear the salmon, oiled side down. Do not attempt to move the salmon until a crisp golden surface has formed, at which point the salmon will lift easily out of the pan.

3 Place in a roasting dish and bake in a preheated oven at 200°C/400°F/Gas 6 for 3-5 minutes, depending on the thickness of the salmon, until just cooked. The salmon should be firm to touch, yet with a pearly pinkness in the middle.

4 Pour the fish stock and lemon juice into a pan and add the star anise. Bring to the boil and reduce by half. Whisk in the chilled butter, a little at a time, to thicken the sauce and give it a gloss. Remove the star anise and season to taste.

5 Roll up the sorrel leaves and shred finely with a sharp knife. Stir quickly into the sauce and check the seasoning. Add a little sugar if necessary. To serve, pour the sauce around the salmon and serve immediately else the sauce will start to lose its colour.

Potted Morecambe Bay Shrimps

If possible, use freshly caught, whole shrimps and cook them yourself in boiling salted water for about 1 minute. If not, buy them from a specialist who boils his own on a daily basis.

Serves 8

1 litre/1¼ pints whole, freshly caught shrimps
75g/3oz unsalted butter
1 blade mace, broken
freshly grated nutmeg
¼ teaspoon cayenne pepper or hot chilli sauce
juice of ½ lemon
freshly ground black pepper
¼ teaspoon caster sugar
clarified butter to preserve

1 Shell the shrimps to give you about 600ml/1 pint of shelled shrimps.

2 Melt the unsalted butter slowly with the piece of mace, nutmeg and cayenne pepper or hot chilli sauce to blend the flavours. Add the shrimps, lemon juice, pepper and sugar and heat through, stirring gently. Remove the mace.

3 Divide between about 8 tiny ramekins and pack down with the back of a spoon. Chill in the refrigerator.

4 When chilled, pour a thin film of clarified butter over the shrimps.

5 Serve the potted shrimps with a salad and some good bread.

A trip to the seaside

If you can get to Morecambe Bay, be sure to buy some of the famous small brown shrimps. They really are the best shrimps for this recipe. Morecambe Bay even has a royal charter to supply shrimps to Her Majesty The Queen. There has been a shrimp industry in Morecambe Bay for over a hundred years, but people also visit Morecambe Bay for its famous, beautiful sunsets.

Steamed Mussels and Scallions in a Cream and Rosemary Sauce

This dish is lovely served with some country bread to mop up the sauce or, for a change, put the mussels and sauce into a prebaked pastry case and serve with a salad for a light lunch.

1.15kg/2½ lb fresh mussels
300ml/10fl oz fish stock
150ml/5fl oz double cream
2 garlic cloves, chopped
2 stems fresh rosemary, chopped
12 scallions or spring onions, chopped
2 tomatoes, skinned, seeded and chopped
salt and freshly ground black pepper
¼ teaspoon sugar
1 tablespoon fresh chives, finely chopped

1 Wash and scrub the mussels. Discard any which are broken. If any of the mussels are open, give them a sharp tap on the work surface. If the mussel is alive it will close of its own accord. Any which remain open are dead and should be discarded.

2 Heat the fish stock in a large, shallow pan until bubbling. Add the mussels. You will need to cook them in about 3 or 4 batches in a shallow layer. It is important to cook the mussels quickly and to remove them from the stock as soon as the shells open, so that they do not become tough. Throw away any mussels that do not open. Remove the mussels from the shells and save to one side.

3 Pour the cooking stock and any stock in the shells through a fine sieve to remove any grit or bits of shell. Pour into a wide shallow pan and add the cream, garlic and rosemary. Reduce to concentrate the flavours and to caramelise the cream slightly to give it a nutty flavour.

4 Add the scallions or spring onions and cook for a minute or so. Add the tomato flesh and the mussels and heat through.

5 Season with lots of freshly ground black pepper, the sugar and a little salt if needed. Remember that the mussel juices will be salty so do taste first. Serve sprinkled with the freshly chopped chives.

Pickled Squab Pigeon with Walnut Oil

2 oven-ready squab pigeons
1 bay leaf, quartered
4 sprigs fresh thyme
150ml/5fl oz brown chicken stock
1 stick celery, finely chopped
4 spring onions, finely chopped
1 small carrot, finely chopped
1 small courgette, finely chopped
½ small red pepper, finely chopped
½ small yellow pepper, finely chopped
300ml/10fl oz walnut oil
2 tablespoons dry Oloroso sherry
2 tablespoons balsamic vinegar
1 tablespoon walnut halves, shelled, blanched and skinned
salt and freshly ground black pepper
selection of salad leaves, optional

1 Cut down either side of the pigeon breast bone and carefully remove the breasts. Make a lengthways cut under each breast and insert a piece of bay leaf and a sprig of thyme. Remove the skin.

2 Heat the chicken stock in a large pan and poach the pigeon breasts gently for 2-3 minutes on each side. The pigeon should still be quite pink in the middle. Remove the pigeons from the stock.

3 To prepare the marinade, fry all the vegetables in a pan with a little of the walnut oil. Do not overcook the vegetables – they should retain their colour and remain crisp. Remove the vegetables to a plate.

4 In a new pan, reduce the sherry and vinegar by about half. Add the stock, remaining walnut oil, walnuts and seasoning and whisk until blended.

5 Pour the marinade into a deep container and add the pigeon breasts and vegetables. Make sure that the pigeon breasts are completely submerged, and then cool and refrigerate overnight.

6 Serve the pigeon, sliced thinly, with a little of the marinade and vegetables. Garnish with a few salad leaves if liked.

Salad of Chicken Livers with Beetroot Dressing

1 small cooked beetroot
2 tablespoons chicken stock
2 sprigs fresh thyme
55ml/2fl oz extra virgin olive oil
1 tablespoon pink peppercorns
salt and freshly ground black pepper
pinch of caster sugar
350g/12oz fresh chicken livers, trimmed
25g/1oz unsalted butter
1 tablespoon pine kernels
2 tablespoons Madeira
selection of salad leaves

1 Liquidise the beetroot with the stock and heat gently in a pan with the thyme, olive oil and peppercorns. Whisk well and check the seasoning. Add a pinch of caster sugar if required.

2 Ensure that the chicken livers are thoroughly trimmed of skin, veins and sinew and season. Heat a cast iron pan or skillet, add the butter and fry the livers briskly for about 1 minute. Remove the livers and keep warm.

3 Add the pine kernels to the butter and brown lightly. Add the Madeira and whisk to make a sauce.

4 To serve, arrange the salad leaves in the centre of four plates and place the livers on top. Pour the sauce over the livers and drizzle the salad with the beetroot dressing.

The first recipe book

The earliest British cookery book was The Forme of Cury, *which was written in the 14th century by the cooks of Richard II.*

Devilled Kidneys on Parsnip Purée

250g/8oz potatoes, peeled and cut into pieces
675g/1½ lb parsnips, peeled and cut into pieces
55g/2oz unsalted butter
grated fresh nutmeg
3 tablespoons double cream
salt and freshly ground black pepper
25g/1oz butter
8 lamb's kidneys, skinned and sliced
2 tablespoons red wine
1 tablespoon red wine vinegar
2 teaspoons tomato purée
3 teaspoons wholegrain mustard
1 teaspoon soy sauce
2 teaspoons Worcester sauce
pinch of sugar
1 tablespoon freshly chopped parsley or chives to garnish

1 Boil the potatoes and parsnips in two separate pans of salted water until cooked. Drain well.

2 Mash the potatoes and parsnips by hand. Do not use a blender or food processor as this spoils the texture. Add the unsalted butter, nutmeg and cream and beat well to make a fluffy purée. Season to taste.

3 Heat the butter in a large pan and sauté the kidneys for 1 minute on each side. Add the wine and wine vinegar and reduce by half.

4 Add the tomato purée, mustard, soy and Worcester sauces and stir well, cooking for a further 2-3 minutes. The kidneys should still be just pink. Check the seasoning and add a pinch of sugar and a dash more Worcester sauce if necessary.

5 Serve the kidneys on the parsnip purée with the sauce poured round. Garnish with freshly chopped parsley or chives.

MAIN COURSES

Fillet of Cod with Parsley and Lemon Crust

*Baked Lakeland Char with Gooseberry
and Sweet Cicely Sauce*

Whitby Fish Pie

Roast Free-Range Chicken with Forcemeat Balls

Pheasants Wrapped in Bacon

Roast Saddle of Hare

Roast Beef with Yorkshire Pudding

Braised Oxtail with Cinnamon

Pot Roasted Leg of Spring Lamb

Fillet of Cod with Parsley and Lemon Crust

The recipe for Harry Ramsden's famous batter is, of course, a well-kept secret!
But why not try this delicious recipe instead?

900g/2lb thick fillet of cod
salt and freshly ground black pepper
zest of 2 lemons
2 garlic cloves, finely chopped
6 tablespoons parsley, freshly chopped
75g/3oz fresh breadcrumbs
3 tablespoons extra virgin olive oil
675g/1½ lb small spinach leaves
extra virgin olive oil for frying

1 Skin the fillet and very carefully remove all the bones. Wash the fish, pat dry and cut into 4 pieces. Season with salt and pepper.

2 Mix the lemon zest, chopped garlic and parsley.

3 Put the breadcrumbs into a frying pan and add the olive oil, stirring and cooking until the crumbs bind together. Add the lemon mixture to the crumbs.

4 Press the crumb mixture firmly into the cod fillets, and place the crumbed fillets on a baking sheet or in a shallow roasting tin.

5 Roast in a preheated oven at 200°C/400°F/Gas 6 for 5-7 minutes, until the fish feels firm and the crumb crusts are crispy and golden. Rest the fish in a warm place for a few minutes.

6 Meanwhile, wash the spinach leaves thoroughly and shake dry. Heat a little olive oil in a large frying pan and quickly stir fry the spinach for a few seconds until the leaves wilt. Season very lightly with salt.

7 Serve the cod on the spinach with seasonal vegetables.

Did you know?

Did you know that a cod can weigh up to 100 pounds and that in some countries,
cods' tongues and cheeks are considered great delicacies?

Baked Lakeland Char with Gooseberry and Sweet Cicely Sauce

Char is a freshwater fish related to salmon and is found in the cold waters of the North, especially the Lake District. This recipe would work just as well with an oily fish such as mackerel or trout.

4 char, each weighing about
225g/8oz, headed, gutted
and cleaned

2 shallots, peeled and
finely chopped

salt and freshly ground
black pepper

1 bulb of Florence fennel,
cut into quarters

zest cut from 1 lemon

2 pieces star anise

½ teaspoon black
peppercorns, crushed

300ml/10fl oz dry white wine
or a mix of wine and water

*for the gooseberry and sweet
cicely sauce:*

225g/8oz gooseberries

55g/2oz caster sugar

90ml/3fl oz cooking liquid
from the baked fish

2 stems sweet cicely

55g/2oz unsalted butter

salt and freshly ground
black pepper

1 Wash the fish, inside and out, and pat dry. Put the shallot inside the fish and season with salt and pepper. Lay the fish and fennel quarters in a shallow oven-proof dish. There should be room for the fish and fennel quarters to fit snugly in a single layer. Season lightly.

2 Add the lemon zest, star anise and crushed peppercorns to the dish.

3 Heat up the wine or wine and water mixture and pour over the fish and fennel. Cover the dish with foil and bake in a preheated oven at 200°C/400°F/Gas 6 for about 20 minutes until the fish and fennel are cooked.

4 Remove from the oven and pour off about 90ml/3fl oz of the cooking liquid. Keep the fish in a warm place whilst you make the sauce.

5 Cook the gooseberries with the sugar in the fish liquid until soft. Add the sweet cicely stems and leaves until they wilt and then immediately liquidise the sauce to keep the colour fresh and the flavour intense.

6 Sieve into a clean pan. Season and then whisk in the butter to blend the flavours and give the sauce a gloss. Taste and adjust the seasoning if necessary. Drain the fish and serve with a piece of fennel and the sauce poured round.

Whitby Fish Pie

You can use any mix of white fish for this dish, so long as it is very fresh and a good buy.
I like to use cod and monkfish although I have made it with plaice, Scarborough
woof or whiting. A handful of fresh prawns or some crabmeat also make
excellent additions.

125g/4oz finnan haddock, skin and bone removed

675g/1½ lb of any mix of white fish, skin and bone removed

salt and freshly ground black pepper

2 tablespoons parsley, freshly chopped

600ml/1 pint double cream

1 fat garlic clove, peeled and crushed

1 teaspoon tomato purée

zest and juice from 1 lemon

½ teaspoon caster sugar

600g/1¼ lb cooked potato, sliced

15g/½oz unsalted butter

1 Cut the haddock and white fish into large bite-sized pieces. Remember it will shrink on cooking.

2 Season well and sprinkle with the chopped parsley. Put in a 1¾ litre/3 pint straight sided oven-proof dish, such as a soufflé dish. Sit this on a baking sheet as the sauce has a tendency to bubble over the sides of the dish.

3 In a wide based pan, bring the cream to the boil. Add the garlic, tomato purée, lemon zest and juice and the caster sugar. Simmer until the cream forms a thickened, reduced and lightly caramelised sauce. Taste and season carefully. Remember that the haddock will add saltiness to the dish.

4 Pour the sauce over the fish and top with layered slices of potato. Dot with small pieces of the unsalted butter.

5 Bake in a preheated oven at 200°C/400°F/Gas 6 for about 15 minutes until the potato is golden brown and the fish cooked.

Roast Free-Range Chicken with Forcemeat Balls

Do seek out free-range chickens for this recipe – the superb flavour will be reward enough.

1 small onion
1 leek
1 small carrot
1 stick celery
salt and freshly ground black pepper
2 x 1kg/2lb 2oz free-range chickens
4 or 5 stems of fresh thyme
1 nodule of fresh root ginger, peeled and cut into matchsticks
55g/2oz unsalted butter, softened

for the sauce:
1 glass red wine
1 tablespoon unsalted butter
fresh lemon juice

1 Wash the vegetables leaving the skins on. Chop roughly and put in the base of a roasting dish large enough to hold both chickens. Season.

2 Wash and dry the chickens and, with the point of a small sharp knife, make incisions all over the chickens and push in small pieces of thyme and ginger. Gently lift the skin away from the flesh and spread the softened butter over the breasts and under the skin. Pull the skin back into place. Season the chickens inside and out.

3 Sit the chickens, breast side down, on top of the vegetables in the roasting dish. This allows the juices to spread down from the back of the chickens into the breasts and keeps them moist.

4 Roast in a preheated oven at 220°C/425°F/Gas 7 for 30 minutes. Turn the chickens on their backs and continue roasting for about another 10-15 minutes until the skin is crisp and the juices run clear.

5 Remove the chickens from the roasting dish and rest in a warm place whilst you make the sauce. Carefully pour off as much fat as possible from the roasting dish and then use the trivet of browned vegetables and the chicken juices in the dish as the base for your sauce.

6 Deglaze the pan with the red wine and reduce until concentrated in flavour then pass through a sieve into a clean pan and swirl in the unsalted butter. If the sauce needs livening up a bit, add a squeeze of fresh lemon juice. Serve the chickens with the sauce and Forcemeat Balls.

for the Forcemeat Balls:
175g/6oz pork fillet, well trimmed
175g/6oz game or chicken livers, trimmed
1 shallot, peeled
25g/1oz fresh white breadcrumbs
salt and freshly ground black pepper
1 tablespoon fresh thyme leaves
1 tablespoon chives, freshly chopped
2 tablespoons parsley, freshly chopped
1 Cox's apple, peeled, cored and finely diced
2 teaspoons plain flour
2 tablespoons olive oil

1 Chop the pork, livers and shallot very finely in a food processor.

2 Add the breadcrumbs and seasoning and process again. Stir in the herbs and apple and bind together by hand.

3 Fry a small piece of the mixture in a pan to enable you to taste and adjust the seasoning. When seasoned to your liking, form the rest of the mixture into walnut sized balls and roll in flour.

4 Heat the olive oil and fry the forcemeat balls until golden, shaking them round in the pan until cooked through.

A good old fry-up

What do you think of as the quintessential English dish? I guess that most people would say Roast Beef and Yorkshire Pudding or Fish and Chips. But the earliest dish was probably Bacon and Eggs, harking back to the days when almost every household would have owned pigs and hens.

Pheasants Wrapped in Bacon

This is a very easy-going dish which can be made in advance. The addition of pig's trotter is not mandatory but I find it gives the sauce a lovely stickiness and richness.

1 brace pheasants	2 carrots
3 sprigs fresh thyme	150ml/5fl oz ruby port
salt and freshly ground black pepper	300ml/10fl oz chicken or game stock
6 slices streaky bacon	½ bottle red wine (such as Rhône or similar)
55g/2oz butter	1 fresh bay leaf
1 pig's trotter (optional)	1 cinnamon stick
1 celeriac	175g/6oz green seedless grapes
1 onion	

1 Take the breasts and legs off the pheasants. Lift the skin and tuck in pieces of thyme. Season with salt and freshly ground black pepper. Cover the pieces of pheasant with bacon and tie on with string.

2 Heat the butter in a wide, shallow pan and sear the pieces of pheasant on all sides. Remove the pheasant to a roasting dish.

3 If using, cut the trotter into 4 pieces and sear until brown. Add to the roasting dish.

4 Fry the vegetables in the same pan to colour them and add to the roasting dish.

5 Deglaze the frying pan with the port and stock and then pour into the roasting dish. Reduce the red wine in the frying pan by a third and add to the roasting dish with the bay leaf, cinnamon stick and any remaining thyme.

6 Baste the pheasant pieces and roast, uncovered, bacon sides up at 200°C/400°F/Gas 6 for about 30 minutes, basting occasionally. Remove the breasts and keep warm. Continue cooking the legs for a further 15-20 minutes until they are tender and the juices run clear.

7 Return the breasts to the roasting dish and remove the bay leaf and cinnamon stick. Remove the pheasant, trotter pieces and celeriac to a serving dish. Sieve the remaining contents of the roasting dish into a clean pan. Whisk and check the seasoning.

8 Add the seedless grapes to the sauce and heat through. Pour over and around the pheasant, trotter and celeriac.

Roast Saddle of Hare

If you buy the whole hare, use the forelegs to make a game stock for the sauce and save the back legs to casserole for another meal. Ask your game dealer to save some of the blood for you to make a liaison which you can use to thicken the sauce.

Serves 2

1 saddle of hare, trimmed	salt and freshly ground black pepper
1 garlic clove, crushed	
8 juniper berries, crushed	55g/2oz unsalted butter
zest from 1 lemon, finely grated	300ml/5fl oz game stock
	2 tablespoons Madeira
2 tablespoons parsley, freshly chopped	2 tablespoons blood
1 tablespoon chives, freshly chopped	

1 Stand the saddle of hare on a board with the backbone uppermost. Using the point of a sharp knife, cut down into the flesh either side of the backbone to form a pocket on each side.

2 Mix together the garlic, juniper, lemon zest and herbs and season. Pack the herb mixture into the pockets. Season the saddle and smear with about a quarter of the butter.

3 Heat a heavy based frying pan until it is evenly hot. Sear the saddle in the pan on all sides to seal in the juices and colour the meat.

4 Put into a roasting dish and roast in a preheated oven at 230°C/450°F/Gas 8 for 4-5 minutes. Remove from the oven and leave to rest in a warm place for a further 10 minutes to settle the juices and tenderise the meat.

5 At this point, reduce the stock with the Madeira and whisk in the blood and remaining butter until thickened.

6 To serve, cut down through the pockets and along the ribs to remove the two fillets from the saddle. Slice diagonally against the grain and arrange with the sauce poured around.

This is delicious served with Parsnip Purée (page 17) and Spiced Red Cabbage (page 36). Forcemeat Balls (page 23) would also make a good accompaniment.

Roast Beef with Yorkshire Pudding

Order your sirloin on the bone and then have it boned and rolled for ease of carving, saving the bones to use as a trivet for the joint. For a 2.7kg/6lb boneless joint you will need to order an 3.6kg/8lb piece of sirloin.

This serves 6-8 people with plenty left over for cold cuts for another meal.

2.7kg/6lb piece of sirloin, boned and rolled, bones reserved

3 fat garlic cloves

3 sprigs fresh thyme

salt and freshly ground black pepper

1 onion, roughly chopped

1 tablespoon plain flour

1 wine glass red wine

300ml/10fl oz beef stock

1 Wipe the beef with a clean, damp cloth and let it stand at room temperature for an hour or so.

2 Cut the garlic into fine slivers and break the thyme into tiny sprigs. With the point of a knife, make small deep cuts all over the surface of the beef. Insert a sliver of garlic and a sprig of thyme in each cut, pushing them well into the joint with the knife. Season the beef with salt and freshly ground black pepper.

3 Heat a roasting tin over a flame and seal the beef on all sides. Remove from tin.

4 Put the bones and onion in a roasting dish and, using them as a trivet, sit the sirloin of beef on top. Roast skin side up, in a preheated oven at 230°C/450°F/Gas 8 for 20 minutes until the beef has browned, basting from time to time.

5 Turn down the oven temperature to 220°C/425°F/Gas 7 and continue roasting for a further 50 minutes to 1 hour 10 minutes until the beef is medium rare. To check, insert a skewer into the middle of the joint. Hold for a count of ten and then touch your top lip with the point of the skewer. If it is warm and the juices run deep pink, it is done. (For well done beef, the skewer will be hot and the juices almost clear.)

6 Remove the joint from the roasting dish and set in a warm place for ½ hour to settle the joint, before carving.

7 To make the gravy, pour away all but about 2 tablespoons of the beef dripping. Make sure you leave behind any meaty bits and the onion. Remove the bones and keep on one side.

8 Sprinkle the flour into the dish to absorb the beef juices. Gradually add the red wine, scraping up all the meaty juices and crusty bits stuck to the roasting dish. Gradually whisk in the stock and bring to the boil.

9 Pour in any juices which have seeped from the beef. Add the bones back to the gravy and continue to bubble away to remove as much flavour from the bones as possible. Check the seasoning. Strain into a gravy boat to serve.

for the Yorkshire Pudding:

Yorkshire Puddings should be crisp, meaty and light as air. Make the batter earlier in the day and let it stand to give a really light result. Do not be tempted to use extra egg as this will give your puddings a stodgy texture. Traditionally, the roast meat juices would be allowed to drip onto the pudding as it was cooking. I use beef dripping to cook the puddings which gives a similar effect.

3 rounded teaspoons plain flour

¼ level teaspoon salt

1 large egg

2 tablespoons milk

150ml/5fl oz cold water

2-3 tablespoons meaty beef dripping

1 While the beef is resting, turn the oven temperature up to 220°C/425°F/Gas 7. Use either a 28x18cm/11x7in roasting tin or a 12 hole tart tin. Individual puddings in tart tins rise better and look nicer, but are not traditional. Prove the roasting tin first by heating for 10 minutes in a very hot oven, which prevents the puddings from sticking. Yorkshire puddings are very simple to make, but it is important that the oven and the dripping are very hot so that steam is produced to make the puddings rise.

2 Sieve the flour and salt into a bowl. Make a well in the centre and drop in the whole egg, the milk and half the water. Using a teaspoon, gradually draw in the flour from the sides into the liquid, blending as you go, to keep the mixture smooth and free from lumps. Whisk in the rest of the cold water using a balloon whisk until the batter resembles thin cream. Add a little extra water if the batter seems too thick. Strain into a jug.

3 When the oven is very hot, pour the dripping into the heated pudding tins and heat again until sizzling. Give the batter a quick whisk and then pour onto the hot fat to fill to the top of the tins. Bake the puddings for 16-20 minutes until well risen and crisp and golden. Serve surrounding the Roast Beef.

Braised Oxtail with Cinnamon

If possible, cook the oxtail the day before it is required. This is so it can be well chilled and the layer of fat that rises to the surface can be removed. Ask your butcher to chop the oxtails into pieces for you.

2 oxtails, cut into pieces	1.2 litres/2 pints rich beef stock
2 tablespoons seasoned flour	3 sticks cinnamon, broken into pieces
knob of butter	
1 onion, chopped	3 bay leaves
2 sticks celery, chopped	1 teaspoon black peppercorns
2 medium carrots, chopped	5-6 sprigs thyme
150ml/5fl oz ruby port	salt and freshly ground black pepper
1 bottle red wine (a full-bodied Rhône would be good)	1 strip of orange zest

1 Trim the oxtail pieces of any excess fat and wash. Toss in the seasoned flour and shake off any excess.

2 Melt a knob of butter in a heavy bottomed pan or frying pan. Add the oxtail and sear brown on all sides. Remove with slotted spoon to a deep oven-proof casserole dish.

3 Brown the vegetables in the pan and then add to the casserole.

4 Add the port to the pan and reduce until sticky, stirring constantly to scrape up any sediment. Gradually add the wine and bring to the boil. Boil hard for about 10 minutes to drive off the alcohol.

5 Add the stock, cinnamon, bay leaves, peppercorns, thyme, salt and pepper and strip of orange zest and return to the boil. Add to the oxtail casserole, cover and cook in preheated oven at 150°C/300°F/Gas 2 for 3½-4 hours, until the meat is falling from the bones.

6 At this point the casserole could be refrigerated overnight to allow the fat to solidify, and then be removed. If serving the same day, remove the oxtail from the casserole with a slotted spoon. Strain the casserole juices into a clean pan. Bring the sauce to the boil and season to taste. Skim off as much fat as possible. The sauce should be deep in colour, rich and unctuous.

7 Reheat the oxtail in a separate pan with a little sauce poured over. Serve the oxtail with the sauce poured over and with mashed potatoes.

Pot Roasted Leg of Spring Lamb

1 leg of lamb, about 2kg/4lb, boned and rolled, bones reserved

salt and freshly ground black pepper

3 stems fresh rosemary

55g/2oz unsalted butter, chilled

1 onion

1 carrot

1 leek

1 stick celery

half a bottle light red wine

1 bay leaf

1 Lightly salt the lamb bones and trimmings and place in a roasting dish. Roast in a preheated oven at 200°C/400°F/Gas 6 for about 20 minutes until browned.

2 Make incisions in the lamb with a small sharp knife and insert tiny sprigs of rosemary in each incision. Season with salt and pepper. Heat half of the butter in a heavy pan or skillet and seal the lamb on all sides.

3 Wash the vegetables but leave the skins on (the natural dye in the vegetable skins will darken and colour the cooking liquid). Chop roughly.

4 Add the vegetables and cook until brown. Reserve 1 glass of wine. Gradually add the rest of the wine and bring to the boil. Add the bay leaf and season lightly.

5 Pour the vegetables and wine into the roasting dish with the bones. Place the lamb on top of the vegetables and return to the oven for 45-50 minutes. Baste occasionally during cooking.

6 To test the lamb, insert a skewer into the thickest part of the meat and hold it there for a count of 10. Hold the skewer to your lower lip. If it is hot, the lamb is cooked. Remove from the dish and rest in a warm place while making the sauce.

7 Carefully pour off any excess fat in the roasting dish. Pour the reserved glass of wine over the vegetables and bones and deglaze, scraping up any meaty bits. Boil until reduced and then add the lamb stock and any remaining rosemary. Reduce by half and then pass through a sieve into a clean saucepan. Whisk in the remaining butter to thicken the sauce and give it a gloss. Adjust seasoning if necessary.

VEGETABLES

Mushy Peas with Mint Sauce

Potato and Lovage Gratin

Bubble and Squeak

Roasted Parsnips with Ginger

Braised Root Vegetables with Winter Savory

Spiced Red Cabbage with Apple and Cinnamon

Braised Leeks with Bacon and Walnuts

Mushy Peas with Mint Sauce

*While Harry Ramsden's are world famous for their Mushy Peas, a traditional
alternative is to serve them with mint sauce. In the North of England, mint
sauce is traditionally made with malt vinegar, although it could be made
just as well with distilled white vinegar or wine vinegar. Ideally, you
need to start this dish the day before.*

225g/8oz dried peas

½ level teaspoon bicarbonate of soda

15g/½oz unsalted butter

salt and freshly ground black pepper

generous handful of fresh mint

caster sugar

1 level tablespoon boiling water

2-3 tablespoons malt vinegar

1 In a large basin, soak the peas overnight (or for at least four hours) in three
times their volume of cold water, with the bicarbonate of soda. This helps to
break down the peas and also keeps them green.

2 Rinse the peas well and put into a medium saucepan and cover with cold
water. Bring to the boil and then reduce the heat to simmer for approximately
1½-2 hours stirring from time to time, until the peas are cooked and have
fallen to a softened mush. If they appear too wet, continue cooking over a low
heat to drive off any excess moisture, but take care to keep stirring, to prevent
them burning on the base of the pan.

3 Beat in the butter, salt and freshly ground black pepper to taste.

4 To make the mint sauce, strip the mint leaves from the stems. Put on a
chopping board and sprinkle with sugar. This makes chopping the mint
easier. Using a sharp knife, chop until fairly fine.

5 Scoop into a serving bowl and pour on the boiling water and malt vinegar
and stir. Add the mint and mix thoroughly. Serve with the Mushy Peas.

Fancy some tomato ketchup?

*Ketchup, as we know it today, is a blend of tomatoes, sugar, salt, vinegar and spices.
But the original ketchup dates back to the 17th century when it was made
with spicy, pickled fish!*

Potato and Lovage Gratin

Lovage has been used since Greek and Roman times for everything from a seasoning, to curing indigestion, to making a love potion. If you cannot get hold of lovage, you could use celery leaves or a few sprigs of rosemary.

750g/1½ lb waxy potatoes, such as Firs Pink, peeled and thinly sliced
12 lovage leaves, chopped
1 egg
300ml/10fl oz double cream
scraping of fresh nutmeg
salt and freshly ground black pepper

1 Layer the potatoes and lovage leaves in a gratin dish or oven-proof shallow baking dish.

2 Beat together the egg, double cream, nutmeg and seasoning and pour over the potato.

3 Bake in a preheated oven at 180°C/350°F/Gas 4 for approximately 45 minutes to 1 hour until the top is a glazed golden brown. Test with a skewer or the tip of a knife to see if the potatoes are cooked.

Sooty goes to Harry Ramsden's

Did you know that Harry Corbett, of Sooty fame, was Harry Ramsden's nephew? He often used to play dance tunes on the piano outside Harry Ramsden's in Guiseley. When Harry 'retired', he opened a new fish and chip shop in Shipley, and it was Sooty that cut the ribbon!

Bubble and Squeak

This is traditionally served on Boxing Day in order to use up all the left-over vegetables from the previous day's excesses! You can change the ingredients to suit whatever vegetables you have available.

550g/1¼ lb good mashing potatoes, peeled and chopped
25g/1oz unsalted butter
285g/10oz dark green cabbage (about half a small one)
1 small garlic clove, crushed
nutmeg, freshly grated
salt and freshly ground black pepper
1 tablespoon sunflower oil

---

1 Cook the potatoes in a saucepan of boiling salted water until soft. Drain well, and mash with half the butter.

2 Remove and discard the outer leaves and core from the cabbage, and shred the leaves very finely.

3 Melt the remaining butter in a large frying pan, add the cabbage and garlic, and stir-fry until soft.

4 Mix the cabbage into the mashed potatoes, adding grated nutmeg to taste. Season with salt and pepper.

5 Form into four patty shapes. Heat the oil in the frying pan and fry the patties for a few minutes on each side until golden. Serve piping hot.

Famous customers at Harry Ramsden's (1)

A quick glance through the visiting book at Harry Ramsden's in Guiseley proves that everyone loves fish and chips. Jeffrey Archer, Margaret Thatcher, Michael Foot and Sir Jimmy Savile are just a few of the famous faces that have dined at Harry's.

Roasted Parsnips with Ginger

A mixture of fats is used in this dish – butter for the flavour it imparts and vegetable oil to raise the roasting temperature and prevent the butter burning.

1kg/2lb 2oz parsnips, peeled and cut into even-sized pieces
2 teaspoons ground ginger
55g/2oz unsalted butter
3 tablespoons vegetable oil
salt

1 Sprinkle the parsnip pieces with the ginger and roll them around until they are covered.

2 Heat a flame- and oven-proof dish or roasting dish on the hob. Add the butter and oil and heat until hazy and hot. Add the parsnip pieces and turn them round in the fats to coat them.

3 Lightly sprinkle with salt. Roast for about 20-25 minutes in a preheated oven at 220°C/425°F/Gas 7 until golden and cooked through. Test with a skewer to make sure the parsnips are cooked.

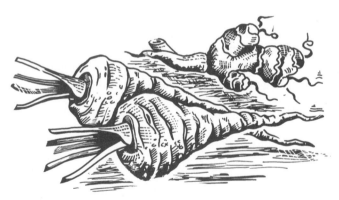

Famous customers at Harry Ramsden's (2)

Cricketers from nearby Headingley often visit Harry Ramsden's. Two of Harry's most regular pre-war customers were Hedley Verity and Bill Bowes, the great bowling duo. Brian Close grew up near the White Cross restaurant and, when older, often ate at Harry Ramsden's after a game at Headingley.

Braised Root Vegetables with Winter Savory

There are two types of savory: winter and summer. It is a close relation of mint, and has a flavour and aroma that is a cross between thyme and mint.

55g/2oz beef dripping
1 celeriac, peeled and chopped
3 carrots, peeled and chopped
4 leeks, peeled and chopped
12 shallots, peeled and chopped
2 parsnips, peeled and chopped
1 tablespoon brown sugar
300ml/10fl oz vegetable stock
1 teaspoon salt
6 sprigs winter savory
chives or parsley, chopped

1 Heat the dripping in a large frying pan and fry the vegetables briskly on all sides. Sprinkle the brown sugar over the vegetables and allow to caramelise slightly.

2 Add the stock, salt and winter savory to the pan and bring to the boil. Pour into an oven-proof dish.

3 Roast in a preheated oven at 200°C/400°F/Gas 6 for about 20 minutes until the vegetables are cooked and are a golden colour. Serve the vegetables in the baking dish, sprinkled with a few chopped chives or a tablespoon of chopped parsley.

Spiced Red Cabbage with Apple and Cinnamon

This is a very easy-going dish which can be made in advance and reheated.
It will keep warm without any harm, so is very useful for entertaining.
I have also frozen it successfully.

1 large onion, finely chopped
4 tablespoons olive oil
3 Cox's apples, peeled, cored and diced small
1 small red cabbage, shredded
2 tablespoons Amontillado sherry
2 tablespoons red wine vinegar
3 level tablespoons brown sugar
grated nutmeg
2 broken sticks cinnamon
salt and freshly ground black pepper

1 Fry the onion in the olive oil and, when softened, add the apple and red cabbage.

2 Add the sherry and wine vinegar, and reduce a little.

3 Add the brown sugar and allow to dissolve. Add the nutmeg and cinnamon and season to taste.

4 Simmer gently for 1½ hours or so until all the flavours have amalgamated, the cabbage has cooked and most of the liquid has evaporated, leaving a syrupy aromatic residue around the cabbage. Check the seasoning, remove the cinnamon sticks and serve.

And that's a fact

The biggest single order for fish and chips that Harry Ramsden's has ever received was 490 portions from an army unit. The longest single order was the Gas Board during a major gas leak when Harry Ramsden's was asked to supply 180 portions on the hour, every hour for 5 hours. One gentleman used to drive to the restaurant from London in his Rolls Royce every Sunday throughout the summer for Sunday lunch.

Braised Leeks with Bacon and Walnuts

8 thin leeks, trimmed and well washed

4 rashers streaky bacon, chopped

salt and freshly ground black pepper

15g/½oz unsalted butter

1 shallot, peeled and finely chopped

4 tomatoes, skinned, deseeded and chopped

300ml/5fl oz chicken or vegetable stock

2 fresh bay leaves

2 tablespoons broken walnut pieces

1 tablespoon walnut oil

1 Cut the leeks in half if necessary, so that they will fit in a single layer in an oven-proof gratin or baking dish.

2 In a wide shallow pan or deep-sided frying pan, dry fry the streaky bacon until the fat flows and the bacon becomes crispy. Remove the bacon from the pan and dry on kitchen paper.

3 Lightly fry the leeks in the bacon fat, until just coloured and then remove and lay them in the gratin dish. Season lightly.

4 Add the butter to the pan and fry the shallot in the bacon fat and butter until golden. Add the chopped tomato, chicken or vegetable stock, bay leaves and seasoning. Pour over the leeks.

5 Heat the walnuts in a separate pan with the walnut oil and bacon pieces. Add to the leeks.

6 Cover the dish with foil and bake in a preheated oven at 180°C/350°F/Gas 4 for approximately 30 minutes until the leeks are tender. Serve the leeks in the gratin dish with the cooking liquid.

PUDDINGS AND DESSERTS

Gooseberry and Elderflower Crumble

Foolproof Custard

Bilberry and Apple Pie

All Butter Shortcrust Pastry

Baked Treacle and Ginger Pudding

Apple Brown Betty

Vanilla Custard Tart

Queen of Puddings

Rhubarb and Ginger Fool

Gooseberry and Elderflower Crumble

900g/2lb gooseberries, topped and tailed
225g/8oz caster sugar
4 elderflower heads (umbrels), washed and dried
90g/3½oz unsalted butter
175g/6oz plain flour
pinch of salt
25g/1oz hazelnuts, chopped

1 Place the gooseberries in a buttered 1¼ litre/2 pint oven-proof dish and sprinkle with 150g/5oz of the caster sugar. Tuck the elderflowers amongst the fruit.

2 In a mixing bowl, rub the butter into the flour and salt until it resembles fine breadcrumbs.

3 Stir in the remaining sugar and the chopped hazelnuts.

4 Working from the outer edges towards the middle, spoon the topping evenly over the fruit. This helps to prevent the juices rising up over the topping from the sides. When it is spread evenly, firm the crumbs down with the back of a spoon and then mark lines across with a fork to help make the top crispy.

5 Bake in a preheated oven at 200°C/400°F/Gas 6 for 40-45 minutes until the top is crispy and golden brown and the gooseberries tender. Serve hot or cold with custard or crème fraîche.

Harry Ramsden's cricketing history

Harry Ramsden, like virtually every other Yorkshireman, loved his cricket. Harry named his White Cross home Larwood House, expressing his admiration for the Nottingham and England fast bowler after the Bodyline Tour to Australia of 1932-33. Freddie Trueman, the great Yorkshire fast bowler, flew over to the first international Harry Ramsden's in Hong Kong to celebrate the serving of Theakston's bitter beer.

Foolproof Custard

*Try to use free-range eggs for this custard for an excellent colour and flavour.
The trick of adding a small amount of cornflour to the custard prevents the eggs
from curdling and it doesn't affect the flavour. Should the custard look like curdling
during reheating, quickly whisk in a tablespoon of double cream. This is a sure fire
way of saving the custard – I know, I've done it many times!*

1 vanilla pod
600ml/1 pint double cream
5 egg yolks
1 level teaspoon cornflour
1 tablespoon caster sugar

1 Split the vanilla pod in half lengthways and scrape out the seeds.

2 Put the seeds and double cream in a saucepan. Add the pod and mix well.

3 Whisk the egg yolks, cornflour and sugar together in a bowl. Bring the
vanilla cream to boiling point and remove the pod. Allow the cream to rise in
the pan, then pour quickly onto the egg mixture, whisking continuously until
the mixture thickens.

4 Pass the custard through a fine sieve – there you have it – quick, Foolproof
Custard!

An apple pie without the cheese is like a kiss without a squeeze (Proverbs)

*Apple puddings have always been firm favourites in the British Isles.
We have Apple Batter Pudding, Apple Amber Pudding, Apple Charlotte,
Apple Crumble, Apple Dumplings, Apple Flan and Baked Apples to name
but a few, but none is more popular than Apple Pie, whether served
with custard, cream or traditional Cheddar cheese.*

Bilberry and Apple Pie

One of the joys of midsummer each year is collecting wild bilberries on the moors. It is a painstaking and delicate job since the bushes grow low and the fruits are born singly and can easily be crushed during picking. If you haven't picked enough for a deep filling, try layering them in a pie with apples, as I've suggested here.

Serves 6-8 generously

1 quantity of All Butter Shortcrust Pastry (page 42)
450g/1lb Granny Smith apples, peeled, cored and sliced thinly
225g/8oz bilberries
75g/3oz caster sugar
beaten egg and milk to glaze

1 Roll out half of the pastry to fit the base of a 20cm/8in pie plate. Layer the apples, bilberries and sugar in the dish. The fruit should be piled up high as it collapses considerably when cooked.

2 Moisten the pastry rim. Roll out the remaining pastry then carefully cover the fruit. Knock the edges together and, using the back of a knife and your forefinger and thumb, crimp round the edges to make a decorative finish. Make decorative cuts in the top to allow the steam to escape.

3 Glaze the top of the pastry with either a little beaten egg and milk (an egg wash) or water and caster sugar to make a crusty finish.

4 Bake in the middle of a preheated oven at 200°C/400°F/Gas 6 for approximately 1 hour until the fruit is tender and the pastry crisp and golden brown. The exact time depends on the depth of fruit (you will have to test it with a skewer).

All Butter Shortcrust Pastry

2 egg yolks
1½ teaspoons lemon juice
3 tablespoons cold water
350g/12oz plain flour
¼ level teaspoon salt
75g/3oz caster sugar
225g/8oz unsalted butter, diced

1 Beat together the yolks, lemon juice and water and chill in a refrigerator to thicken slightly.

2 Sieve the flour, salt and sugar together and rub in the butter until the mixture resembles fine breadcrumbs. Keep your hands cool and use only your fingertips to prevent the butter melting and making the dough heavy.

3 Add all the liquid in one go and stir until it starts to bind, then finish by hand. Knead gently and wrap in a plastic wrap or Clingfilm. Chill in a refrigerator to rest and firm up. Use as required.

Record breaker

Harry Ramsden's has broken the world record on four occasions for selling the most portions of fish and chips in a day. The first record was set on 7th July 1952 when Harry celebrated 21 years at Guiseley. Fish and chips were sold at the old 1912 prices – just 1½d per portion. In 1988 to celebrate Harry Ramsden's Diamond Jubilee, the record was broken again, this time with the price being just 2 pence per portion. In 1992, Harry Ramden's in Glasgow served an amazing 11,964 portions, breaking the record for the third time. On Good Friday 5th April 1996, Harry Ramsden's in Melbourne broke the record again when they served 12,105 portions.

Baked Treacle and Ginger Pudding

Make certain that all the ingredients are warm before you start,
to ensure the quickest and best results.

butter, caster sugar and ground
almonds to prepare the moulds

100g/4oz unsalted butter,
softened

100g/4oz caster sugar

1 large egg

100g/4oz self-raising flour

½ level teaspoon baking powder

pinch of salt

1 level teaspoon ground ginger

5 tablespoons golden syrup

1 piece stem ginger, chopped

1 tablespoon ginger syrup taken
from the stem ginger jar

juice of ½ lemon

1 Lightly grease four individual pudding moulds and dredge each with caster sugar and ground almonds. Tap out any excess.

2 Cream the butter and sugar until pale and fluffy.

3 Beat the egg and gradually add to the creamed mixture, beating well after each addition.

4 Mix together the flour, baking powder, salt and ground ginger. Gently fold into the butter mixture, using a balloon whisk or tablespoon. Add two tablespoons of the golden syrup. The mixture should have a very soft, dropping consistency.

5 Divide between the prepared moulds, tapping the moulds lightly on your work surface to settle the mixture evenly and to avoid air bubbles.

6 Bake in a preheated oven at 170°C/325°F/Gas 3 for about 15-20 minutes until well risen and golden. The puddings should feel as firm in the middle as at the edges and should have shrunk away slightly from the sides of the moulds.

7 To make the sauce, put the stem ginger, ginger syrup, remaining golden syrup and lemon juice into a small pan and bring to the boil. Simmer to amalgamate the flavours and reduce slightly.

8 When the puddings are turned out, pour the ginger sauce around to serve.

Apple Brown Betty

*This is a pudding which was popular in country areas in the nineteenth century.
The traditional recipe used apples although I can remember making it with
damsons as a child.*

600g/1¼ lb Bramley apples, peeled, cored and sliced thinly
100g/4oz demerara sugar
grated zest and juice of 1 lemon
1 cinnamon stick, broken into 5 or 6 pieces
75g/3oz unsalted butter
175g/6oz fresh brown breadcrumbs
1 tablespoon extra demerara sugar

1 Mix together the apple slices, demerara sugar, the zest and juice of the
lemon and the pieces of cinnamon stick.

2 Melt the butter in a heavy based frying pan and tip in the breadcrumbs.
Cook over a medium heat, stirring constantly with a wooden spoon until all
the butter has been absorbed and the crumbs are golden in colour.

3 Layer the apple and crumbs in a buttered, oven-proof 1¼ litre/2 pint dish
finishing with a layer of crumbs. Press down with the back of a spoon.
Sprinkle the tablespoon of extra demerara sugar on top.

4 Bake in the centre of a preheated oven at 180°C/350°F/Gas 4 for about 45-
50 minutes until the apples are soft and the top is crispy and brown. You will
need to test the apples with a skewer. If the top is brown before the apple is
cooked, cover the surface lightly with a piece of baking parchment or foil. Do
not tuck it round as this will spoil the crispness of the topping. Serve with
clotted cream.

A squeeze of lemon juice?

*Warm lemons yield more juice, so don't try to squeeze a lemon straight
from the refrigerator. If you only want a little squeeze of lemon juice, prick it
with a fork or small knife. The holes will be large enough for some juice to
squeeze out, but will seal afterwards.*

Vanilla Custard Tart

This is a very simple, traditional dessert where the quality of the ingredients really counts. Be sure to use unsalted butter for the pastry, fresh, free-range eggs and double cream for the custard. It's rich and velvety and a little will go a long way.

250g/9oz All Butter Shortcrust Pastry (page 42)
1 egg white
5 free-range eggs
25g/1oz caster sugar
450ml/15fl oz single cream
150ml/5fl oz double cream
1 whole vanilla pod
nutmeg, freshly grated
icing sugar to dredge

1 Roll out the pastry to line an 18cm/7in deep-sided fluted, flan tin. Line it with foil and baking beans and bake it blind in a preheated oven at 190°C/375°F/Gas 5 for 15 minutes. Remove the foil and beans. Reduce the oven temperature to 150°C/300°F/Gas 2 and dry out for a further 10 minutes. Do not turn off the oven, as you will need it at this temperature later.

2 Brush the inside of the pastry case with beaten egg white while it is still warm to form a protective crust. This will seal the pastry and keep it crisp when filled with the custard.

3 In a large bowl, whisk the eggs with the sugar, single and double cream.

4 Split the vanilla pod in half lengthways, scrape out the seeds and add them to the custard mixture. (I suggest you save the pod and pop it into a bowl of caster sugar to flavour it for later use.) Sieve the custard into a clean bowl.

5 Stand the pastry-lined flan tin on a baking sheet. Pour the custard into the pastry case to reach to the top of the pastry. Grate the fresh nutmeg lightly over the surface.

6 Carefully transfer to the centre of the oven and bake for 1-1¼ hours at 150°C/300°F/Gas 2, turning the oven down to 140°C/275°F/Gas 1 after 30 minutes. The tart will still be slightly wobbly in the centre but will continue to cook as it cools down. When cool, dredge with icing sugar.

Queen of Puddings

Raspberries are a favourite allotment fruit here in the North and this meringue-topped pudding is particularly popular. You use the egg yolks to make the Foolproof Custard which you need for this recipe – a thrifty Northern device!

55g/2oz fresh white breadcrumbs
grated zest of 1 lemon
600ml/1 pint Foolproof Custard (page 40)
3 tablespoons raspberry jam
1 tablespoon cold water
175g/6oz raspberries
5 egg whites
pinch of salt
4 tablespoons caster sugar
1 tablespoon flaked almonds (optional)

1 Sprinkle the breadcrumbs and grated lemon zest into a 1 litre/1¼ pint oven-proof serving dish and pour the custard over them. Cool, then chill in the refrigerator for 2 hours.

2 Warm the jam with the water and pass through a fine sieve to remove the seeds. Spread the jam over the custard. Top with the raspberries.

3 Whisk the egg whites with a pinch of salt until they form stiff peaks. Whisk in 3 tablespoons of the sugar and bring back to form stiff, glossy peaks.

4 Pile the meringue on top of the custard in rough peaks – do not attempt to level the meringue, but make sure the custard is completely covered.

5 Scatter with the remaining caster sugar and decorate with flaked almonds if you like. Bake in a preheated oven at 120°C/250°F/Gas ½ for 25-30 minutes until the top of the meringue is crisp with light golden peaks.

6 Serve hot or cold. If you have extra raspberries, purée them with a little icing sugar and serve as a sharp sauce with the pudding.

A regional variation

Manchester has its own version of Queen of Puddings, called Manchester Pudding. The meringue is spread directly onto the pudding without the additional layer of jam and the two are baked together.

Rhubarb and Ginger Fool

150ml/5fl oz double cream
1 teaspoon icing sugar
600g/1¼ lb early season forced rhubarb
3 tablespoons water
225g/8oz caster sugar
2 or 3 drops pink food colouring if needed
2 pieces stem ginger, sliced thinly into strips
150ml/5fl oz Foolproof Custard (page 40), chilled

1 Whisk the cream with the icing sugar until firm, but not stiff and dry. Chill.

2 Top, tail and wash the rhubarb but leave the pink skins on. Cook the rhubarb in a wide shallow pan with the water and caster sugar until softened to a pulp. If the colour is not pink enough from the skins, add 2 or 3 drops of colouring to enhance it. (It should be pale pink but as the rhubarb gets older the resultant purée is less pink and may need a little help!) Press the purée through a very coarse sieve to remove any stringy bits but do try to leave some texture in the fruit.

3 Stir the ginger into the rhubarb and chill well.

4 Place alternate spoonfuls of the custard, cream and fruit purée in a wide bowl. Using a spatula, draw them lightly together to give a pink, yellow and white marbled effect.

5 Spoon into pretty stemmed glasses. Serve with shortbread fingers.

HIGH TEA

High Tea is very different from Afternoon Tea. It is the main meal eaten at around 6pm in the North and Scotland, and is usually followed by a light supper later in the evening. The dishes that follow in this chapter are a real taste of tradition, and represent many of the Northern regional ingredients and produce.

Rum-Roasted Gammon Ham with Demerara Sugar

Kedgeree

Parsley Fish Cakes

Soused Herrings

Potato, Stilton, Apple and Celery Salad

Bacon and Thyme Girdle Scones

Yorkshire Parkin

Singin' Hinnies

Cut and Come Again Cake

Yorkshire Curd Tart

Madeira Tipsy Trifle

Gooseberry Chutney

Rum-Roasted Gammon Ham with Demerara Sugar

You will need to start this recipe the evening before. The cinnamon used for this recipe is best ground in an electric grinder, but can be done with a pestle and mortar. There really is a difference in flavour in grinding your own – do try it.

Serves 8

3kg/6lb piece of gammon ham, boned (corner cut, if possible)
4 tablespoons dark rum
6 tablespoons demerara sugar
zest and juice of 2 limes
2 tablespoons grain mustard
1 small cinnamon stick, ground
freshly ground black pepper

1 Soak the ham overnight in cold water. The next day, drain and pat dry.

2 Sit the piece of ham in a large pan and cover it with cold water. Cover with a lid. Bring quickly to the boil and then simmer gently for 1½ hours.

3 Whilst the ham is cooking, mix together all the remaining ingredients. Remove the ham from the water and drain. With a sharp knife, and taking care because of the heat, peel off the skin, leaving the fat behind. Score a diamond pattern all over the fat.

4 Put the ham in a dry roasting tin and then spread the glaze generously over the surface. Leave for as long as possible, but at least 25-35 minutes, for the flavours to impart. Roast in a preheated oven at 220°C/425°F/Gas 7 for approximately 30-45 minutes to finish cooking the ham, crisp the fat and allow the glaze to permeate the flesh. If serving hot, allow to stand for 20 minutes before carving.

Kedgeree

If you prefer your kedgeree less spicy, try cooking the rice with nutmeg only. This gives a much milder, creamy kedgeree.

625g/1¼ lb finnan haddock	1 level teaspoon salt
55g/2oz butter	3 tablespoons double cream
½ onion, very finely chopped	juice of 1 lemon
4 cardamom pods, crushed	1 tablespoon chopped coriander
2 teaspoons cumin seeds, freshly ground	salt and freshly ground black pepper
1 teaspoon garam masala	yolks of 2 hard boiled eggs, finely sieved
1 teaspoon turmeric	coriander sprigs, to garnish
100g/4oz basmati rice	

1 Lightly cook the haddock in a little warm water with a knob of the butter for 3-4 minutes and drain. Remove the skin and bones and lightly flake the fish leaving the pieces quite large.

2 Fry the onion in the rest of the butter. Add all the spices and cook for 2-3 minutes to soften the onion and release the flavours.

3 Add the rice and stir to coat. Add water to cover and the salt. Bring to the boil and cook gently until the water is absorbed. Keep stirring to prevent from sticking and keep adding water until rice is cooked and all the liquid is absorbed.

4 Stir in the flaked haddock and cream and heat through. Add the lemon juice to give it a zip and stir through the chopped coriander. Season to taste.

5 Serve topped with the sieved egg yolks and some extra sprigs of coriander.

Origins

Finnan haddock was originally fished in Findon, Scotland, a small fishing village near Aberdeen. The name now refers to haddock that has been lightly salted, smoked and partially boned. Originally, it would have been smoked over peat fires. Kedgeree was originally a spiced East Indian dish of rice, lentils and onions. It was anglicised in the 18th century when the English added flaked smoked fish, boiled egg and cream.

Parsley Fish Cakes

350g/12oz cooked potatoes
25g/1oz butter, melted
salt and freshly ground black pepper
grated zest and juice of 1 lemon
175g/6oz salmon fillet, skinned
175g/6oz cod or woof fillet, skinned
4 tablespoons parsley, freshly chopped
2 tablespoons chives, freshly chopped
6 spring onions, peeled and sliced finely
1 egg, beaten
6 tablespoons fine white breadcrumbs
4 tablespoons sunflower oil
25g/1oz unsalted butter

1 Mash the potatoes with the melted butter, salt and pepper.

2 Heat a little water and a splash of lemon juice in a shallow pan and lightly poach the salmon and cod or woof until just cooked. Season and remove the fish and flake.

3 Put the mashed potato and fish into a large mixing bowl, add the chopped herbs, lemon zest and spring onions and mix thoroughly. Taste and adjust the seasoning if necessary.

4 Take teaspoonfuls of the mixture and roll into about 8 balls. Flatten the top and sides with a palette knife to form small fish cakes.

5 Pour the beaten egg onto a plate and the breadcrumbs onto a second plate. Dip the fish cakes first into the beaten egg and then in the breadcrumbs to coat. Pat smooth with the palette knife.

6 Heat a cast iron or heavy based frying pan. Heat half the sunflower oil and half the butter together and fry the fish cakes on all sides until crisp, golden and hot. You will need to cook them in two batches, keeping the first batch in a warm place whilst cooking the second batch. Drain on absorbent paper and serve with lemon wedges or perhaps a parsley sauce.

Soused Herrings

*Not to be confused with rollmops, soused herrings are infinitely more subtle
and are a firm North Country favourite for High Tea.*

2 tablespoons white wine vinegar
150ml/¼ pint dry white wine
1 shallot, chopped
1 garlic clove, sliced
300ml/5fl oz fish stock
1 teaspoon black peppercorns
½ teaspoon salt
4 star anise
½ teaspoon coriander seeds

½ teaspoon fennel seeds
2 bay leaves
2 or 3 sprigs of fennel leaf
½ red jalapeno chilli pepper,
deseeded
½ teaspoon sugar
4 tablespoons olive oil
6 x 225g/8oz herrings, filleted

1 In a wide based pan, start to reduce the wine vinegar and wine over a high
heat. Add the shallot and garlic and further reduce the wine by about half.

2 Add the fish stock, the seasoning, all the aromatics, including the chilli,
and the sugar. Bring to the boil and boil rapidly for about 10 minutes until the
flavours are amalgamated and concentrated slightly and the acidity has
mellowed. Add the oil, stir and remove from the heat.

3 Roll up the fillets from the thick end to the tail end (they don't seem to roll
properly and hold their shape the other way round). Stand them on end, coil
upright, in a small, deep, oven-proof dish. Pour the marinade over them to
come three-quarters of the way up the fish.

4 Cover with foil and bake in a preheated oven at 200°C/400°F/Gas 6 for
about 4-5 minutes, longer if the herrings are larger, until the fish is opaque.
Remove from the oven and remove the foil. Allow to cool in the marinade to
allow the fish to take up the flavours of the aromatics. Serve warm.

Harry Ramsden's worldwide

*Harry Ramsden's opened its first international restaurant in August 1992 in
Hong Kong. The 200 seater restaurant and take-away have been modelled on
the original Guiseley restaurant, with most of the ingredients being exported
from the United Kingdom. Since then, Harry Ramsden's have opened
restaurants in Singapore, Saudi Arabia and Australia.*

Potato, Stilton, Apple and Celery Salad

This is a great salad if you want to use up leftover new potatoes.
The amount is not critical – just use what you have.

3 tablespoons walnut oil
1 tablespoon sherry vinegar
salt and freshly ground black pepper
1 garlic clove, crushed
1 tablespoon chives, freshly chopped
150-175g/5-6oz new potatoes, peeled, boiled and chopped
2 crisp red eating apples, cored and sliced
100g/4oz green seedless grapes
175g/6oz Stilton, cubed
1 bunch celery, sliced
celery leaves, to garnish

1 In a large mixing bowl, beat together the walnut oil, sherry vinegar and seasoning. Add the garlic and chives.

2 Add all the remaining ingredients and toss gently to coat. Serve in an attractive dish and garnish with celery leaves.

Time for tea

High tea would not be complete without a pot of freshly brewed tea. Tea is one of the world's most popular beverages, with Ireland being the biggest fans, drinking on average eight cups a day, per person. The world's best-selling brands are Lipton's and Brooke Bond and the most expensive tea is Makaibari Flowery Tippy Golden Flowery Orange Pekoe, which in 1992 sold for £240 per kilogram.

Bacon and Thyme Girdle Scones

Girdle is a regional variation of the word 'griddle'.

6 rashers streaky bacon, derinded and cut into ½ cm/¼ in pieces
225g/8oz plain flour
3 level teaspoons baking powder
1 level teaspoon powdered mustard
salt and freshly ground black pepper
55g/2oz butter
2 teaspoons thyme leaves, freshly picked
150ml/5fl oz mixture of milk and water (about half and half)

1 Fry or grill the bacon until crisp, and leave to cool.

2 Sieve together the flour, baking powder, mustard and seasoning. Rub in the butter until the mixture resembles breadcrumbs. Stir in the thyme and bacon. Add the liquid and stir with a knife to form a soft dough.

3 Turn the dough out onto a lightly floured surface and knead very gently. Handle as little and as lightly as possible to keep the girdle scones light. Roll into a cylinder shape about 7-10cm/3-4in in diameter and cut into ½cm/¼in thick slices.

4 Gently heat a griddle or cast iron frying pan to an even heat. Grease, and cook the scones for 5-6 minutes on each side until golden and cooked through. Serve hot with butter.

A cricket tea menu

For a traditional cricket tea, you will need:
1 dozen tuna and cucumber sandwiches
1 dozen ham and tomato rolls
2 dozen chicken legs
a large plate of bacon and thyme scones
1 gammon ham and 1 large pork pie
1 large dish of potato salad
lots of crisps
tomato and gooseberry chutney
2 large fruit cakes
2 Yorkshire parkins
and a very large urn of Yorkshire tea!

Yorkshire Parkin

*A type of gingerbread peculiar to Northern England, Yorkshire Parkin has
a knobbly texture and the rich, dark taste of black treacle.*

175g/6oz self-raising flour
2 level teaspoons ground ginger
1 level teaspoon cinnamon
½ level teaspoon baking powder
½ level teaspoon bicarbonate of soda
pinch of salt
175g/6oz rolled oats
175g/6oz unsalted butter
75g/3oz golden syrup
55g/2oz black treacle
55g/2oz soft brown sugar
2 eggs
2 tablespoons milk

1 Sieve together the first six ingredients into a mixing bowl, and add the
rolled oats.

2 In a saucepan, melt together the butter, golden syrup, black treacle and
soft brown sugar over a warm heat and stir until well mixed. Pour into the
bowl of dry ingredients.

3 Beat the eggs and milk and add them to the mixing bowl. Draw the dry
ingredients into the wet ingredients with a wooden spoon and blend together
to make a stiff batter.

4 Pour into a prepared tin and bake for approximately 1¼ hours in a
preheated oven at 150°C/300°F/Gas 2 until well risen, dark brown and firm
in the middle. Cut into squares to serve.

Gingerbread during the time of King Arthur

*Gingerbread dates back to the Middle Ages when it was given as a 'favour'
to jousting knights, by their ladies. It was often intricately shaped,
and sometimes decorated with gold leaf.*

Singin' Hinnies

Singin' hinnies are sweet griddle cakes which are best served hot, split and buttered. Hinnie is the North East endearment meaning 'honey'. If you do not have a griddle or the top of an Aga to cook on, just use a cast iron frying pan or a heavy based non-stick frying pan. They will do the job just as well.

225g/8oz plain flour
½ level teaspoon baking powder
¼ level teaspoon bicarbonate of soda
¼ teaspoon salt
100g/4oz unsalted butter, diced
100g/4oz mixed dried fruit
2 teaspoons honey
8 tablespoons milk
lard or mutton fat to grease the griddle

1 Sift the flour, baking powder, bicarbonate of soda and salt into a mixing bowl.

2 Rub the butter into the flour mixture and add the dried fruit.

3 Dissolve the honey in the milk and stir into the mixture using a knife, adding extra milk if needed to make a soft dough.

4 Roll out to about ½cm/¼in thickness and, using a round cutter, cut 8 or 9 griddle scones about 5cm/2in across.

5 Heat the griddle until evenly warm and grease with lard or mutton fat. Cook the griddle cakes first on one side until golden brown and starting to puff up. Turn with a palette knife and cook on the other side. Keep turning and cooking for about 16-20 minutes until cooked through. Serve warm in a napkin with lots of butter.

Cut and Come Again Cake

Cut and come again cake is unique to the British Isles. The probable reason for the name is that the cake dries during baking, so it was necessary to leave the cake to soften or 'come again'. It stays lovely and moist for at least a week. It also freezes brilliantly.

350g/12oz unsalted butter, softened

350g/12oz caster sugar

6 large eggs, lightly whisked

450g/1lb self-raising flour

55g/2oz ground almonds

2 level teaspoons baking powder

½ level teaspoon ground cinnamon

½ level teaspoon freshly grated nutmeg

3 tablespoons milk

3 tablespoons water

75g/3oz brazil nuts, chopped

75g/3oz hazelnuts, chopped

75g/3oz walnuts, chopped

150g/5oz dried apricots, chopped

for the topping:

225g/8oz apricot jam, warmed

55g/2oz of each kind of nuts

1 Cream together the butter and sugar. Gradually beat in the eggs, a little at a time.

2 Sift together the flour, ground almonds, baking powder, ground cinnamon and grated nutmeg and fold into the creamed mixture, adding milk and water as required. Fold the nuts and apricots into the mixture.

3 Spoon the mixture into a 20cm/8in round cake tin double-lined with parchment or greaseproof paper and bake in a preheated oven at 140°C/275°F/Gas 1 for about 2-2¼ hours. The cake should be well risen and golden, be firm in the middle and have shrunk slightly from the sides of the tin. Cool on a wire rack.

4 Warm the apricot jam in a saucepan with 4 tablespoons of cold water, stirring to blend. Sieve out any pieces of fruit. If the jam has a particularly stiff set, you may need to add another tablespoon of water. If the jam you have chosen seems too sweet, a squeeze of lemon juice will soon liven it up.

5 When cold, brush the top of the cake with the warmed apricot glaze. Arrange nuts decoratively on the cake. Brush over again with the apricot glaze to give them a gloss and also to fix them to the cake.

Yorkshire Curd Tart

175g/6oz All Butter Shortcrust Pastry (page 42)
55g/2oz unsalted butter, softened
55g/2oz caster sugar
225g/8oz cream or curd cheese
2 eggs, beaten
25g/1oz sultanas
25g/1oz dried apricots, diced
1 tablespoon white breadcrumbs
1 level teaspoon ground mixed spice
2 tablespoons apricot jam
caster sugar to dredge

1 Line a 22cm/9in tart tin with the pastry and bake blind, in a preheated oven at 190°C/375°F/Gas 5 for 15 minutes. Remove the foil and beans. Reduce the oven temperature to 150°C/300°F/Gas 2 and dry out for a further 10 minutes.

2 Beat together the butter and caster sugar until light and fluffy. Beat in the cream cheese.

3 Add the eggs a little at a time, beating well after each addition.

4 Mix together the fruits, breadcrumbs and spice and fold gently into the curd mixture.

5 Spread the apricot jam in the pastry case and then top with the curd mixture. Spread evenly.

6 Reheat the oven to 190°C/375°F/Gas 5 and then bake the tart for approximately 20 minutes until well risen. Reduce the oven temperature to 170°C/325°F/Gas 3 and continue baking for about 30 minutes until the top is golden and quite firm to the touch. The curd tart will continue to firm up as it cools.

7 Remove to a cooling rack and dredge the tart lightly with caster sugar. Serve warm.

Madeira Tipsy Trifle

This recipe makes enough sponge for two trifles, so freeze the second for later.

175g/6oz self-raising flour
1 level teaspoon baking powder
175g/6oz butter, softened
175g/6oz caster sugar
zest of 1 orange, grated
3 large eggs
225g/8oz raspberries
1 tablespoon cold water
4 tablespoons caster sugar
1 vanilla pod

450ml/15fl oz double cream
2 heaped teaspoons icing sugar
150ml/5fl oz Madeira
2 tablespoons fresh orange juice
1 tablespoon brandy
4 tablespoons jam
1 quantity of Foolproof Custard (page 40)
1 tablespoon flaked almonds, toasted

1 First make the orange flavoured sponge. Sieve the flour and baking powder together. Add the butter, 175g/6oz caster sugar, orange zest and eggs and whisk until the mixture is smooth and a soft dropping consistency.

2 Prepare two 20cm/8in sandwich tins by greasing well with butter and dusting with caster sugar. Divide the mixture between the tins and bake in a preheated oven at 160°C/325°F/Gas 3 for 20-25 minutes until golden and firm in the middle. Turn out onto a wire tray to cool.

3 To make the fruit purée, liquidise together the raspberries, water and 1 tablespoon of caster sugar and sieve to remove the seeds.

4 Split the vanilla pod and scoop the seeds into the double cream.

5 Sieve the icing sugar and add to the cream. Whisk lightly to form a soft floppy consistency which will spread easily.

6 Mix together the Madeira, orange juice, remaining 3 tablespoons of caster sugar and the brandy.

7 To assemble the trifle, slice one sponge in half horizontally and spread thickly with the jam. Sandwich the sponge layers back together, cut the sponge into pieces and arrange in a glass dish. Pour over the Madeira mixture and top with the fruit purée. Spread with the custard, top with the whipped cream mixture, and spread thickly. Decorate with the toasted, flaked almonds.

Gooseberry Chutney

Try to leave the chutney to mature for a few weeks if possible.

Makes about 3 x 450g/1lb jars

1.35kg/3lb gooseberries, topped and tailed
350g/12oz Cox's apples, peeled, cored and chopped
2 large onions, finely chopped
200g/7oz Barbados brown sugar
300ml/10fl oz white wine vinegar
2 cinnamon sticks, broken
1 tablespoon mustard seeds
1 small red chilli, cut in half and deseeded

1 Put the prepared fruits, onion, brown sugar and wine vinegar into a large, heavy based pan and cook over a low heat until the sugar has dissolved. Add the broken cinnamon sticks, mustard seeds and chilli.

2 Bring everything to the boil, stirring from time to time and then simmer for about 1 hour until the mixture is thick and aromatic.

3 Remove the cinnamon and chilli and discard. Pot the chutney into warmed, sterile jars and cover with waxed paper circles immediately. Seal with screw tops whilst warm.

The origin of chutney

Chutney originally came from India, but like many other recipes, such as Kedgeree, is now thought of as typically English. It is delicious served with warm savoury scones, welsh rarebit or, of course, the traditional ploughman's lunch.

INDEX

£2.00 off
your next visit to

Harry Ramsden's

This voucher entitles you to a saving of
£2.00 when you spend £10.00 or more on
your next visit to any Harry Ramsden's
restaurant in the UK and Ireland.

A list of Harry Ramsden's restaurants at
date of publication is shown overleaf.

This offer cannot be used in conjunction
with any other promotional offer.
Photocopies are not valid.
Offer closes 31 December 1998.

Name of Promoter: Harry Ramsden's plc, White Cross,
Guiseley, Leeds LS20 8LZ.

Harry Ramsden's

RESTAURANTS

ENGLAND

Guiseley
White Cross, Guiseley,
Leeds, LS20 8LZ
Tel: 01943 874641

Blackpool
60-63 The Promenade,
Blackpool FY1 4QU
Tel: 01253 294386

Birmingham
1741 Coventry Road,
Yardley, Birmingham
B26 1DS
Tel: 0121 7654646

Bristol
Cribbs Causeway,
Bristol,
Avon BS10 7TQ
Tel: 0117 9594100

Bournemouth
East Beach,
Undercliff Drive,
Bournemouth
BH1 2EZ
Tel: 01202 295818

Exeter
M5 Granada Service
Area, Sandygate,
Exeter EX2 7HF
Tel: 01392 446559

Gateshead
Metro Park West,
Gateshead,
Tyne & Wear
NE11 9XF
Tel: 0191 4602625

Heathrow
Terminal One,
London Heathrow,
Hounslow,
Middlesex TW6 1JH
Tel: 0181 7455022

Hilton Park
Hilton Park Services,
M6 Essington,
Nr. Wolverhampton,
Staffordshire
WV11 2DR
Tel: 01922 412237

Liverpool
Brunswick Way,
Off Sefton Street,
Liverpool L3 4BN
Tel: 0151 7094545

Manchester
1 Water Street,
Castlefield,
Manchester M3 4JU
Tel: 0161 8329144

Nottingham
Riverside Retail Park,
Queens Drive,
Nr Clifton Bridge,
Nottingham NG2 1RT
Tel: 0115 9861304

Oxford
28/31 St Ebbes Street,
Oxford
Tel: 01865 202404

SCOTLAND

Edinburgh
Newhaven Fish Market,
Newhaven Harbour,
Edinburgh EH6 4LU
Tel: 0131 5515566

Glasgow
251 Paisley Road,
Glasgow G5 8RA
Tel: 0141 4293700

WALES

Cardiff
Landsea House,
Stewart Street,
Cardiff Bay CF1 6BW
Tel: 01222 463334

NORTHERN IRELAND

Belfast
Yorkgate Shopping
Centre, Belfast
Tel: 01232 749222

REPUBLIC OF IRELAND

Dublin
Naas Road,
Dublin, Eire
Tel: 00 353 14 600233

Harry Ramsden's also have restaurants in
Hong Kong, Singapore, Saudi Arabia and Australia.